What Happens to the Dog?

By Martha Tolles

Illustrated by Bert Jackson

DOMINIE PRESS
Pearson Learning Group

"That's all the time we have for today, class," she says.

Everyone in the room groans. We all want to read this book.

"I have a surprise for you," Miss Ramirez says. "The author of this book is coming to visit our school in a few days to talk to our class. Our school library has bought a copy of her book so that everyone will have a chance to finish reading it."

I am sure that lots of other kids will want to read the book, too. I'll never be able to read the ending myself. I put up my hand. "Could I buy her book?"

Miss Ramirez makes a sad face. "You could, Josh. But it costs fourteen dollars."

Maybe my mom will give me fourteen dollars.

Chapter Two
I Have to Know

That night at supper, I tell my mom about the book and the author coming to our school. Even my younger sister, Sarah, listens. And I think our little dog, Smokey, is listening, too.

Mom smiles when I finish. "I guess

you really like the story," she says.

"I do. Mom, I have to know what happens to that dog in the story. The coyotes might get him. Couldn't I buy the book? It's only fourteen dollars." I reach down and pet Smokey. "I already have two dollars."

"I could give you my fifty cents," Sarah puts in. "I want to hear the story, too."

But Mom shakes her head. "Sorry, kids. I'd like to hear that story, too. But remember, just last week I bought you computer games and those animal cards. I can't spend any more money right now. How about putting it on your birthday list? Or checking it out of the school library?"

"I'll have to wait a long time." I groan and eat some spaghetti. Then I hang my

hand down so Smokey can lick it. That helps, but not enough.

Then I get an idea.

After supper, I call my friend Andy.

"Do you have any money?" I ask him. "We could go in together and buy that book our teacher is reading to us."

"It's a good story, but I'm saving up for a new computer game," Andy says. "Besides, I only have a dollar."

I hang up, discouraged. Then I get an idea. Maybe I could earn the money! I could have a lemonade stand out in the street. But it's not summer and we don't have any lemons. Then I get a *great* idea.

"Mom, could I make some fudge?" I ask. "You know, the way Grandma used to do when she came to visit. I could sell it to everyone on the street!"

Chapter Three
Make Fudge and Earn Money

Mom and I discuss my plan to make fudge and earn money. She says OK.

"Can I start the fudge now?" I ask.

"Yes," Mom agrees. "I'll do my work right here at the kitchen table." She goes to a class twice a week. "I'll help you

with the hot liquid when the fudge is done," she says.

"When you get that book, will you read it to me?" Sarah asks.

"Sure, Sarah," I say.

I measure out the sugar and the milk and the baking chocolate. While I do that, Sarah hugs and pets Smokey, and tries to get him to wear her doll's hat. He's such a great dog. I'd hate to have anything bad happen to him.

Then Mom turns on the stove, and we put the pot on the burner. We all hang out in the kitchen and watch the fudge slowly simmer and bubble. It smells really good, and I dream of all the money I'll make and the book I'm going to buy.

Then my mom helps me pour the fudge into a pan to cool. It won't be ready for a while.

The next day at school, Miss Ramirez doesn't read *Bert and Baxter* to us.

I'm really disappointed. Instead, she has us make a big poster to welcome the author.

During recess I tell my friend Tyler, "I'm going to sell fudge and make a lot of money. Then I can buy that book."

"Good idea," he says. "Want me to help you?"

"That's OK," I say. "My sister and my mom will probably do that."

That afternoon I set the pan of fudge on the kitchen table. Mom and I cut it into squares. Smokey sniffs around the kitchen floor. Just then we hear a thump and a cry from Sarah's room.

Chapter Four
Poor Smokey

What could have happened to Sarah? We run into her room. She's fallen out of bed and is rubbing her head and crying. Mom hugs her and I pat her and tell her she's going to be OK. She keeps crying.

I say, "Listen, Sarah, I'll give you a

piece of my fudge." She stops crying right away. "Only one piece," I add. "I have to sell the rest so I can buy that book about Baxter and the coyotes."

So then we go out to the kitchen and, oh, what a disaster we see. "Smokey!" I shout. Smokey is up on the kitchen table, eating the fudge. And it's almost gone! How am I going to sell it now?

And worse yet, Mom says, "Oh, no. Chocolate is really bad for dogs. He'll be sick. We have to get him to the vet right away."

On the way to the vet, Smokey is already acting sick.

"Smokey, you bad dog. Why did you eat that fudge?" I'm cuddling him on my lap. I'm not really mad at him, just worried.

He just whimpers and flops his tail.

His stomach looks all puffed out, maybe from all the water he drank before we left. And I feel horrible for leaving that fudge out where he could get it.

"Poor Smokey," Sarah croons.

All that makes me think about that book I want to buy, *Bert and Baxter*.

Does Bert feel as worried about Baxter as I feel about Smokey? I wonder which is worse, to have coyotes after your dog, or to have your dog get sick from eating too much chocolate.

Chapter Five
Whew!

The vet says that chocolate can be bad for a dog's heart, so he gives Smokey something to make him throw up. He says Smokey will be OK. Mom has to pay a big bill, though. But I am so relieved. I go to sleep with a big smile on my face that night. Smokey snuggles up against me.

The next day the author comes to our school. We all rush up to her.

"What happens to Baxter?" we ask. "Do the coyotes get him?" I wish I could buy her book, but with no fudge to sell and no money, I know I can't.

"Oh, I can't give away the ending," she says. "It's better for you to read it."

When she finishes her talk, she says, "Do some of you have pets? You can write stories about them."

Two girls raise their hands. One has a snake who got out of his cage. The other has a bird that can say "crackers." I think about Smokey. Suddenly I want to tell about him eating the fudge. I shoot my hand up in the air. I pour out my whole story. Then at the end, I feel I ought to explain, so I add, "I was going

to sell the fudge so I could buy your book."

"Oh, you were?" The author looks surprised, then pleased. "What a tough time you and your dog had." She glances toward Miss Ramirez. "I'd like to donate an extra copy of my book to your class. Maybe this boy can be the first one to read it."

Miss Ramirez lets me check out the book that day. I guess if you keep trying, even if you make mistakes, things can turn out all right. (And they did for Baxter, too, I found out later when I read the book.)

Whew!